M000023489

The *Christmas* CREED

Enhanced and revised edition of
Cracked Wheat for Christmas

Books by Ted Hindmarsh

The *Christmas* CREED

Enhanced and revised edition of
Cracked Wheat for Christmas

Ted Hindmarsh

Sweetwater Books
An Imprint of Cedar Fort, Inc.
Springville, Utah

This is a work of fiction. The characters, names, incidents, places, and dialogue are products of the author's imagination and are not to be construed as real. The views expressed within this work are the sole responsibility of the author and do not necessarily reflect the position of Cedar Fort, Inc., or any other entity.

ISBN 13: 978-1-59955-519-5

Published by Sweetwater Books, an imprint of Cedar Fort, Inc.
2373 W. 700 S., Springville, UT, 84663
Distributed by Cedar Fort, Inc., www.cedarfort.com

LIBRARY OF CONGRESS CATALOGING-IN-PUBLICATION DATA

Hindmarsh, Ted C. author.
 The Christmas creed / Ted Hindmarsh.
  p. cm.
 Summary: On his way home to New England for the holidays, a snobbish doctor is stranded in a snowstorm and rescued by a poor family with three small children.
 ISBN 978-1-59955-519-5
 1. Christmas--Fiction. I. Title.

PS3558.I4775C73 2011
813'.54--dc22

2010046718

Cover design by Megan Whittier
Cover design © 2011 by Lyle Mortimer

Printed in the United States of America

10 9 8 7 6 5 4 3 2 1

Acknowledgments

My sincere thanks and acknowledgment to:

My supportive readers

Lyle Mortimer and all of my friends
at Cedar Fort Publishing

Shirlene Hindmarsh, my beloved
wife and primary critic and editor.

This book would never have happened
without any of them.

Foreword

Over the many years since the original publication of *Cracked Wheat for Christmas*, I have appreciated the enthusiastic feedback we have received from its readers—most of which has been positive, and all of which has been helpful.

During the past few years, that feedback has taught me that a revisit to the story may be appropriate for the new members of its audience, as well as for its devoted continuing readership.

The goal of this revisit was not to rewrite the story, but to bring it up to date while still preserving all of its endearing qualities and its endorsement of the enchanting ability of the true spirit of Christmas to inspire, uplift, and motivate positive life changes.

I hope you enjoy the revisit as much as I enjoyed crafting it.

—Ted Hindmarsh

Contents

Contents

Chapter 1

Doctor Alexander Pennington III

Finally, following one frustrating delay after another, the shiny new automobile accelerated down the on-ramp to the eastbound Interstate. It was leaving California to bear its owner to his family and associates in New England. (He thought of them as his associates because he wasn't sure they could really be called his friends.)

Thirty-year-old Doctor Alexander Pennington III sat behind the steering wheel of his new status symbol, relieved to be on his way at last. He was looking forward to two full weeks of freedom from the pressures of study, work, and political shenanigans he'd endured for the past several years—efforts that were finally making it possible for him to pay for this marvelous piece of machinery.

Both Doctors Alexander Pennington I and II had expected this of him since his birth, and he knew that each one waited anxiously for a full report. Neither was happy about his choice to work in the West, and even less excited that his primary involvement was research. How can one have a prestigious practice bulging with wealthy patients if all he does is research? To the exclusive New England family of Pennington, Alexander Pennington III knew that temporal success was everything. Wealth and influence must transcend even love for family. He realized that this philosophy may sound cold to the bulk of humanity, but in the Pennington world, where respect was centered on possession and control, it was simply the practical way of doing business.

Oh, Alexander III had been trained well, but he loved his involvement in medical science. He had fought hard to win a position on the research staff of the University that was a renowned leader in the work. It put him in what he considered to be an enviable situation where he could control his time, for the most part, and he wouldn't have to spend his life mollycoddling hypochondriacs and eccentric weirdos.

Doctor Alexander Pennington III was pleased with himself, and now that his salary was beginning to match his ability, Doctors Alexander I and II would, by their own standards, have to be pleased with him too.

The digital clock on the space-age dashboard indicated 6:00 a.m., December 23. He was going home for the holidays. Because of unexpected delays, he was a day late getting away. He probably should have flown, but then he wouldn't have this all-important status symbol along. He was used to functioning on minimal sleep, and if he really pushed it, Alex figured he could still be there for the latter part of Christmas day. But that would still give him two full weeks to display his Pennington stuff.

His sleek machine was eager to run.

Alex was tempted to let it all out, but reason ruled and he set the cruise control to an easy seventy-four miles per hour—a fraction of its potential.

The Interstate curved from south to east to go up and over the low rolling mountains. He was, both literally and figuratively, on his way, and there was nothing in view to stop him.

He'd been too pressed for time to do much serious Christmas shopping, but Alex thought it was probably just as well, since he couldn't possibly cram anything else into his car.

The gifts he had picked up were not anything anyone needed. His selections were mainly chosen to impress: an expensive canned ham, a selection of imported breads, cheeses, and chocolate drink mixes, a basket of assorted fresh fruits, and a three-gallon can of Western Clover Honey for his mother. She loved showy foods and could serve these for the entire next year at her countless teas and gatherings.

There were two gifts that tickled him, though. One was the gold-plated folding hunting knife that he'd picked up for his grandfather. Dr. Alexander I was too old to hunt anymore, but it would bring back memories of the safaris of his youth. And even if it didn't, anything with gold on it would impress him.

The other gift was a huge stuffed bear for his twenty-year-old sister, Keri. Alex knew it was absolutely useless, but she was always accusing him of treating her like a child, so in playful ways, he never missed an opportunity to do just that. He knew she didn't particularly like stuffed animals, so when he saw the huge bear, he had to get it for her. But then, as he was paying for the bear, he saw a wristwatch that he knew she'd think was really cool. His conscience kicked in, and he bought it for her too, to offset the teasing effect of the bear.

Alex grumped inwardly that after what she'd done to him, she didn't even deserve a gift from him this year. He was still fuming that she had dumped all her stuff on him to bring home for her. She was a student at the same university that employed him, but she only came to see him when she needed something. It seemed to him that she was majoring in what he called "socialite science," the same degree he often accused his mother of earning when she went to the same school.

Keri was flying home for Christmas, and when she learned that he was driving, she called and asked if he could take a few things with him that she couldn't squeeze into her bags to get on the airplane. Alex would have surely refused if he had realized what she meant by "a few things."

So she showed up with this big box that just barely fit into the trunk of his car. She said it contained the new ski outfit she'd purchased at Saks the last time she was home. She loved it, of course, but when she got back to school, her roommate's friend had one the exact same color, so of course she couldn't keep it. The box also held several new sweaters she had never worn, but she was sure they would be essential during the holidays. Her bulky blow-dryer was in there too.

Alex had grumped that she was only going to be home for two weeks! But it was clear that she had her agenda, and she pointed out that he was, after all, her big brother who was supposed to be looking after her.

Well, the upshot of this mostly one-sided sibling bantering was that when Keri got all of her things crammed into the car with what he already had packed, the only place for the huge bear was in the passenger seat beside him. No way would his Pennington ego permit him to drive his new status symbol all the way across the country seated beside an oversized stuffed bear—so he covered it with a bed sheet.

To Alex, this long drive home was not just a Christmas holiday with family. It was far more an ideal opportunity to show off his worldly attainments. He felt no real sentiment or understanding of the true meaning of the holiday, nor did he know very much about the One whose birth it celebrated. He was a Pennington. He was young, healthy, and successful, and he was beginning to earn his own substantial income. He was unattached and free, and he liked it that way.

He had no use for marriage. He had everything he wanted, and none of what he didn't want . . . namely, children. He felt uncomfortable when they were around, and they seemed happy to respond in kind. He was well aware that there were some well-placed women who, eligible as he was, had serious designs on him. But they were all so self-centered and possessive. Although he suspected that one of them would eventually wear down his resistance, he was in no hurry. His life was under control and just the way he wanted it, and anyone else who wanted to possess even a little piece of him was out of luck.

For all of his life, Alex brooded, the tenets of The Pennington Creed had been hammered into him. That Creed was the family guide to temporal success, a sort of rephrased version of the law of survival of the fittest. To his knowledge, the five main tenets of the Creed had never been written, but nonetheless, they were vivid in his mind:

GIVING TO CHARITY: Do so only when it can be regarded as an investment that promises great returns. People are poor only because of their own indolence, and giving to them only fuels the fire of their debilitating fever. If they get hungry enough they will work, and work is what they need, not handouts.

CHURCH ATTENDANCE: Okay for social reasons and if it will improve your status in the community and credibility in the marketplace, but never grovel in worship. That is a misplacement of priorities.

FAITH IN GOD: It's all right as long as it isn't overdone, but never let it replace faith in self. It is a sign of weakness and subservience that can be used to great advantage by your adversary.

EMOTION: Keep your heart above your work. Never let it drag through the mire of empathy or pity. Thus exposed, it could only get bruised or broken. And no man with a broken heart can keep the pace.

EATING HABITS: Never eat natural foods like whole wheat, or drink milk still warm from a cow. Though it may be nourishing to the body, it sends subtle signals to the soul that you are ready to be humble and willing to rely on others for part of your existence. And worse, that you might have a need to be taught some things you don't know about humility. In short, the very naturalness of such foods would invalidate every other tenet of the Creed!

The Creed was not too romantic, but it was practical and sound. Alex lived by it devotedly. It was the nearest thing he knew to a religion, and it had been very carefully taught.

Obedience to the Creed had given Alex what he felt was the best of all possible worlds, and all around him he saw examples of what happens when people live otherwise. There were the welfare patients that he and all the other doctors in the state were required to treat without remuneration. They seemed to be the patients who needed the most help, and yet they could never pay. How could people let their lives get so messed up? He called them "the cracked wheat eaters" because that is what they invariably ate.

He freely admitted that he was egotistical and selfish, but he saw these traits as signs of strength, not weakness. He had never given anything that hadn't been a carefully calculated investment with the promise of a healthy return. He hated the greed of society and preferred to practice his in private. He was impatient with slothfulness and imperfection. He wondered why everyone could not be more like him. Though he was very pleased with himself, he couldn't remember ever feeling that way about anyone else. He knew that he was hypercritical and cynical, but he was practical and realistic. He had worked hard to get where he was, and he regarded other people as challenges to be met and conquered.

Oh, he had been carefully trained, and now he was anxious to get on with this next exciting phase of his life. He was on his way! His old mentors in the East would have to be pleased.

Chapter 2

The Incident

The beautiful automobile hummed like the precision instrument it was. The digital dials on the dashboard flashed multi-colored messages that revealed the car's inner secrets. Everything operated at the peak of engineered perfection. As mile after mile of freeway were eaten and spewed out in a continuous ribbon behind, the audio system filled the car's interior with mellow sounds that surrounded the driver and his shrouded overstuffed passenger with an almost liquid quality. Doctor Alexander Pennington III inhaled the aroma of automobile newness and basked in real leather and walnut luxury.

As a skilled surgeon, Alex was surrounded

by the latest tools, but he was still awed by the technology that enwrapped him in this fine automobile. Even though he was zipping through the heart of rural America, with his hands-free cell phone clipped into place, he was still electronically connected to civilization. And with his car's satellite phone at his right hand, he could instantly be in contact with any other location on earth. Easy, free, self-sufficient—this was his style. He could hardly wait to show it off.

As he was cruising along the Interstate, a radio weatherman was warning about an approaching storm. But he was making good time, and he was used to going without sleep. If he kept his pace, he could surely outrun the threat and make it to the East Coast for at least a part of Christmas.

The day, along with the miles, melted into dusk. The headlights automatically snapped on and illuminated the broken white stripe on the roadway's surface. As night approached, the new car purred up a slight incline where the interstate was flanked on either side by sparsely scattered pinion pines and junipers, now visible only as dark shadows on the gentle slopes of the darkening hills.

Alex had long since passed the big cities. The Interstate now forged through some of the least-populated, more mountainous areas of the country. He had been driving for over an hour without passing a roadside business, and his GPS screen showed that the next outpost was still twenty miles in the distance ahead.

From the cutting edge of the headlight illumination, a green off-ramp sign appeared that identified an obscure exit to the right, one mile ahead. It also contained the warning Alex had found to be so plentiful in this part of the country: "No services available."

As the green sign shot past, it was almost as though it tripped an invisible wire that held all of the car's precision systems together. Instantly, the once smooth-running engine began to jerk and sputter. Alex's eyes widened in alarm as red lights lit the dashboard with danger signals. The bright headlights began to dim noticeably, and the audio system faded into silence. Something was terribly wrong.

Alex responded almost instinctively. Not wanting to be stranded on this dark stretch of freeway, he turned right onto the exit as he came to it. The new car stuttered and loped and just barely made it to the access road at the top of the incline where an overpass arched over the Interstate to his left. Then everything went dark and silent as the car jerked to a halt.

In disbelief, Alex slowly relaxed his iron grip on the steering wheel. Everything was ominously quiet. The headlights had gone out, the liquid audio had faded to nothing, the engine had stopped running, and the once-brilliant dashboard had totally faded to black.

Alex fished the keyless ignition pad from his pocket and pressed the engine start button on the dash. Nothing happened. Not a sound.

He opened the door and was startled to see that there wasn't even a dome light. He got out and walked to the front of the car. He was an excellent surgeon, but he was not a mechanic. He tentatively fumbled with the hood latch. He pressed where the salesman had told him to in his new owner operating instructions and it popped open. He lifted the hood. In the darkness he could see nothing amiss. He wiggled the wires and felt the belts and hoses, which were plenty warm, but nothing out of the ordinary. He rubbed his hands together and then shut the hood. He looked around the countryside. All he saw was darkness.

Alex's heart leapt as a semi truck rumbled along the Interstate and under the overpass. He felt an urge to wave and shout, but realized that would be futile. He climbed back into the driver's seat and, just to assure himself, he held the keyless ignition pad up close to the dash and hit the engine start button.

Nothing.

All of the once-precision life had gone out

of his expensive new automobile.

Alex clenched his fist and thumped the steering wheel so hard it stung his hand.

"I paid too much for this puppy to get this kind of treatment," he complained out loud. "Why me?" he yelled with a little flare of temper.

He jammed the keyless pad right next to the button again, and again, there was no response.

With an accustomed reflex, Alex reached for his cell phone. He flipped it open to dial for information to call a tow truck. The call didn't go through. As he watched, the lighted keypad faded to black. With another small fit of frustration, it dawned on him that in his hassle to get ready to leave, he had not charged the battery. It was completely dead.

In near desperation, he grabbed the satellite phone from its cradle. He should be able to call anywhere in the world with this baby. But there was no response. Apparently whatever had messed up the car's electronics had also affected the satellite phone. It slowly dawned on Alex that he was out in the middle of nowhere in arguably the most technologically advanced country on earth, and he was totally cut off from all communication with the outer world. The reality of the situation settled in like a dense fog. Alex had never felt so alone in his life.

Finally, in reluctant defeat, Alex stuffed the keyless pad back into his pocket, grabbed his new leather jacket from where it was stowed behind the giant bear, and climbed from the car. He slammed the door shut with another little flare of temper and hit the lock button on the keyless pad. When nothing happened, He threw his arms in the air, jammed the key into the slot on the door, and locked it manually.

Then he turned again to survey the scene. Except for a faint glow that lingered on the western horizon, the sky was completely dark. Down the incline on the freeway, a car emerged from the blackness, coming from the opposite direction, and zoomed under the overpass. Alex watched it for a long time as its taillights disappeared around a distant bend. Then Dr. Alexander Pennington III pulled on his new leather jacket against a stiffening breeze, and walked down the on-ramp toward the freeway.

The absolute silence was stunning. Alex could feel more than see that some clouds were moving in to obscure the stars. He quivered with an involuntary shiver that was motivated by reasons that went far beyond temperature.

Another semi lumbered into view in the darkness, its running lights flickering in the gloom. Alex's heart leaped. He ran down the on-ramp toward it. He waved his arms and yelled, but the driver obviously couldn't see him in the dark. The truck didn't even slow down. As it whined under the overpass, its exhaust stack belched black smoke that was visible in the brightness of the headlights reflecting from the white concrete of the overpass abutment. The truck's running lights and the whining of its tires on the pavement were gradually absorbed by darkness and distance.

The loneliness was frightening—almost overwhelming.

More headlights came into view. Ah, this was the one. They couldn't help but see him this time. As the car bore down upon him, Alex waved and jumped and yelled, but it didn't even slow down. He was sure the driver saw him. What was this world coming to?

"Keep going, turkey!" he shouted in desperation.

Surely someone will stop eventually, he thought. They have to! It would take all night to walk to the next town.

The wind increased and the temperature was dropping noticeably. The storm he had been trying to outrun was catching up with him. Another car approached from the opposite side of the Interstate. He waved and yelled, but it didn't stop either.

"What a way to treat a guy on Christmas!" Alex mumbled audibly.

He turned the collar of his jacket up against the cold. He paced restlessly back and forth. He looked at his watch—8:00 p.m. He had been stranded for over an hour. At this rate, he would never get home. Would anyone ever stop?

It seemed as though he had waited for hours. Where had all the traffic gone? He checked his watch again. Only 8:20. Those twenty minutes had dragged by sluggishly. This could be a long, cold night.

Think, Alex told himself. There must be a way out of this. He reasoned that maybe he could coast the car down the off-ramp backward. A stranded car would be easier to notice than a man walking in the blackness. Maybe having the car up out of the way in the dark wasn't such a good idea after all.

He walked back to his car, mildly encouraged that at least he had a plan. The electronic door lock didn't respond to the keyless pad, so he unlocked it the old fashioned way with the attached key. He opened the door and slipped behind the wheel. He put the keyless pad up next to the dash and tried the starter button again, just in case. Again, there was no response. He moved the gearshift lever to the neutral position and released the break. The car didn't budge. He got out and tried to push it. No luck.

"Something is drastically wrong with this car," he said incredulously, as if someone were listening.

"Well," he declared to the same imaginary person, "I can't just sit around and do nothing."

He would have to leave the car there and walk to the next town, even if it did take all night. Surely someone would see him walking along the Interstate and pick him up. Maybe even a state trooper.

Once again he locked the car securely, only this time he headed down the on-ramp toward the freeway.

"What was that?" he exclaimed to himself in surprise. Something had drawn his attention up the hill to his left across the highway. He stopped and looked closer. As the wind blew the branches of the trees, he saw what appeared to be a flicker of light. He watched intently. There it was again. It *was* a light! It seemed to be coming from a small depression between some gently sloping hills. His heart beat with encouragement. Maybe he wasn't as far away from people as he thought. He turned around and headed quickly back up the on-ramp. He nearly ran across the overpass in the direction of the light.

A pickup truck rolled by noisily under the overpass, right below him. He hoped he'd made the right decision. That just might have been his ride.

Oh well, no point in staying with the freeway now. The light became more visible, even if only in occasional blinks.

The highway pavement ended at a cattle guard about thirty yards from the overpass.

A dirt road continued up into the hills. He walked along the dirt road for what he estimated to be about a half mile. At one point, his heart jumped into his throat as a mule deer burst from beside the road and thumped off into the darkness.

"Boy, that's enough to wake you right up!" he said aloud as his heart pounded.

Finally, the incline leveled out onto a small flat, right in the middle of which sat a most welcome sight. It was a small house. The one little window he could see had a curtain across it, but a cheery glow came through. The light that had attracted his attention was a bright rural yard light on a tall pole. Beyond the house was what appeared to be an outbuilding—perhaps a barn. Things looked friendly enough, but he wondered what kind of people would deliberately choose to live way out in a remote place like this.

He approached the house, which, though small, appeared to be sturdily built and well kept. He walked up to the porch. A large washtub was hanging on the wall under the porch's cover beside two pairs of antique-looking leather-thonged snowshoes and a coal-oil weather lamp. It looked good to see even these rustic signs of civilization and human life.

He walked up the steps and knocked gently on the sturdy door. Muffled sounds rustled from inside, but no one answered. *The place is so small, surely they heard the knock*, he thought.

He looked around at the surroundings, and involuntarily shuddered again. Snow was beginning to fall, and the cold was even more intense. He reached out and knocked again, only this time with more vigor. Finally the door opened, but only a crack, and Alex was startled to find himself looking into the muzzle of a double-barreled shotgun! The voice of a young boy came from behind the door.

"Who are you? What do you want?"

What a great way to treat a guest! he thought.

"I'm Alex Pennington. My car is stranded down by the freeway. Could I use your phone to call for a tow truck?"

"We don't have a phone! Go away!"

Irritated thoughts filled Alex's mind. *Rotten kid! All kids are the same—rotten!*

"It's cold out here." Alex's voice was rising. "And it's snowing! Can I talk with your mom or dad?

"They're not here!" the voice responded stubbornly. "Go away!"

Alex was tempted to just force the door and go in. Certainly he could overpower a small boy, but that shotgun gave him second thoughts. If the boy became frightened enough, it might not be too good. The boy had probably been well trained. If his folks were not home, he probably was not supposed to let anyone in.

"When will your folks be home?" he asked.

"I don't know. Go away!"

"Look kid, I'm not going to hurt you! I just . . ."

"You look, Mister. I don't want to have to shoot you. Now get off this property!"

"But I don't have anywhere to go. My car is broken! It's cold and snowing," Alex persisted. What else could he do?

"Don't bother us!" the boy threatened. "I'm giving you one minute to be out of the range of this shotgun, and then I'm going to start shooting!"

Us! There must be more than one. Better not push your luck, Alex. No telling what's in there. Rotten kid! Every kid in the world needs a good spanking! Better keep it to yourself!

"Will you at least tell me how far it is to the next town?"

"Twenty miles. You can get a ride at the freeway!"

"Thanks a lot, pal!"

Alex fought for control of his temper. He couldn't blame the kid for doing what he'd been taught to do. Nor could he play around in this weather. Who knew what it was going to do? It felt like it was about to get ugly.

Reason returned. Alex couldn't believe that any parents would leave their kids out here alone for very long. Surely they would return soon. He would walk back to the car and try to keep warm. When the parents did come back they would have to pass right by the car to get home. He would intercept them there and stop frightening the boy and whoever else was in there.

As he walked back along the road, he was amused by the incredible nature of this whole thing. Why him?

He knew the distance was a good half mile. The blowing snow had become a blizzard, and before he reached the car he was soaked.

Another semi rig ghosted slowly along the Interstate below. This time, he could barely see it through the blowing snow. This was going to get worse before it got better. He realized that he had better try to warm up and dry out a little before he tried any other bright ideas. His shivering hand unlocked the car door. He got in and waited.

In his wet clothes, the car felt like a refrigerator. This was not going to work. The temperature dropped steadily, and the wind howled. He couldn't stay here. Again, in desperation, he tried to start the car. Nothing! Not even a click.

Now Alex was genuinely frightened. For the first time in his life he was confronted by a situation he couldn't seem to get a handle on. Freezing to death in his modern status symbol was a very real possibility. His only hope now seemed to be the freeway. No one could refuse a man on foot out in weather like this. He shuddered at the thought of standing on the freeway, but it was either that or the kid with the shotgun.

Whatever was keeping those parents?

His hands and feet were numb. He had to get moving. He checked his watch. It was the only thing that was still working. Ten-thirty. Finally he opened the door to the raging storm, locked the door, and once again headed down the on-ramp. The intensity of the storm gave him second thoughts about trying the kid again. If he wasn't picked up soon it would be all over. If the kid wouldn't let him in, maybe he could make it in the barn. Actually it was a useless thought. He realized that he probably couldn't even make back to the little house. No, slim as they were, his chances were better along the freeway.

He hadn't walked ten steps before he heard an incredible sound. It was a small voice coming from behind him.

"Mister! Mister! Wait!"

He turned into the blizzard and could barely make out the small form that was reaching for his hand.

"Don't try to walk in this," the voice yelled over the storm. "You'll never make it. They will close the highway and you'll never get a ride. Come back to the house. We've changed our minds. You can stay with us!"

Alex wasn't at all sure what was going on, but he wasn't in any position to argue. He'd never had a better-sounding offer in his life! He couldn't see where he was going, so he entrusted himself completely to the little form that was clutching tightly to his hand—a hand that now had no feeling. He blindly followed wherever the form led him.

Chapter 3

The Stewarts

The ordeal seemed like it would never pass, but finally the small house was there. The door opened, and they were inside.

Oh, warmth, light, civilization!

The door shut, and a cozy, orderly room that doubled as a kitchen and a living room instantly replaced the fury of the storm. On the opposite side was a marvelous, beautiful stone fireplace with a cheerfully blazing, inviting fire. Alex had never seen anything that looked so good. Beside the fireplace stood a good-looking boy with neatly trimmed light brown hair. Alex judged him to be ten or eleven years old. He wore a stern look on his handsome face, and he was still holding the shotgun at the ready. The odd thing was that he didn't look too rotten.

The voice of the form at Alex's side spoke.

"It's okay, David. The man was telling the truth. His car is broken. He would have frozen out there. You can put the gun away. He won't hurt us."

As the voice spoke, small hands removed a large work-worn coat and gloves. The scarf about the head and neck fell away and revealed the lovely brown locks of a pretty little girl who was perhaps a year or two older than the boy. She somehow seemed much older and wiser than her years. She turned to Alex.

"Please come over by the fire and get warm. My name is Melissa Stewart, and this is my brother, David. I'm sorry we kept you out there so long, but we had to be sure you were telling the truth. You can never tell these days."

The boy obediently leaned the shotgun in a corner. In what was surely complete trust of his sister's judgment, he extended his hand in a frank but gentlemanly manner. Alex was impressed.

"What's your name?" David asked with surprising frankness.

"I'm Alex Pennington," Alex replied, "and I really appreciate you letting me in. You probably saved my life. I don't know what I would have done if you hadn't . . ."

"Pleased to meet you," the boy interrupted, giving Alex's still tingling hand a vigorous shake.

"Please let me take your coat. I'll hang it up by the fire."

As Alex's numbed mind struggled to bring meaning and reason to the situation, another voice spoke from behind him.

"Would you like a blanket to get you warm, Mr. Penny . . . Penny . . .ton?"

It was an even tinier voice. Alex spun around and looked down into the biggest, most beautiful brown eyes he had ever seen. They belonged to a gorgeous little girl who couldn't have been more than four or five years old. She was dressed in an old but freshly laundered sweatshirt that reached nearly to her tiny bare feet.

My word, there are three of them, he thought.

He bent down to take the blanket she offered.

"Well, thank you, sweetheart," Alex responded. *That sounded awkward*, he thought, but it was the only thing that came to his mind. "You can just call me Alex. What's your name?"

Melissa stepped forward.

"This is our little sister, Emily. We call her Emmy."

"Well, Emmy," Alex said as he wrapped the warm blanket about his shoulders. "You are the most beautiful little person I've ever seen."

"Thank you," Emmy replied politely. "What were you doing out there in the cold, Alex?" she asked.

"Well, my car broke down, and I didn't

have anywhere to go," Alex answered.

He couldn't believe that he was actually having a sensible conversation with children, but he had to admit that these children were remarkable.

"Alex, please sit down in the big chair and take off those wet shoes and socks." Even though it was delivered politely, the suggestion sounded almost like a motherly directive. However, Alex was more than glad to obey this small but authoritative female named Melissa.

"Here, drink this," she continued. "It will warm you up from the inside."

She held out a worn mug that was steaming from something she had dipped from a large kettle sitting on a small cook stove in the corner. It looked like milk. He sipped the liquid. It was warm and tasty. She was right. He felt the first swallow go clear down, warming him all the way.

"What's this?" Alex asked.

"It's warm milk," David answered.

"Why does it taste different than other milk?" Alex asked.

"It doesn't taste any different than always," David answered. "It's fresh. I just got it out of Mabel a few hours ago."

"Mabel?" Alex gulped in surprise.

"Yeah, Mabel, our cow," David said in his straightforward manner.

"Milk still warm from a cow," Alex muttered, almost as if a small recording had come on in his mind. He stared into the cup and then placed it on the hearth of the fireplace. "Thanks very much," he said with an apologetic smile, "but I'm not really very thirsty."

He could tell Melissa knew he didn't like the raw milk. He wasn't doing a great job disguising it.

"Well then, may I fix you some supper?" She asked. "You must be starved after what you've been through."

Alex really didn't want to impose any more on these remarkable little people, but the thought of some warm food inside him did have some appeal.

"What are you serving at this late hour?" he asked.

"I could cook you some nice, hot cracked wheat," came the response.

Cracked wheat, he thought. *This must be some kind of conspiracy.* Alex answered almost by reflex. "No, thank you, Melissa. It's very late and I've caused you enough trouble already."

Alex did genuinely appreciate the offer, but he would never be thirsty enough or cold enough to drink milk still warm from a cow, or hungry enough to eat cracked wheat and send subtle signals to his soul.

Alex's brain was finally able to function again, and it was time he got some answers. Emmy's pretty little mouth opened wide in a lengthy yawn, and the lids of her big eyes were beginning to droop.

Alex checked his watch again. Almost midnight.

"Wow! He said. "I'm really keeping you guys up past your bedtime. Your dad will kill me when he comes home."

"We don't have a dad," said Emmy.

"You don't? Well, where's your Mom?" Alex asked.

He saw Melissa and David exchange anxious glances. "Come on, Emmy," Melissa said, taking her by the hand. "We'd better put you to bed."

"Oh, you guys never let me stay up," Emmy protested as her brother and sister led her into a small bedroom.

It was certain that the two older ones didn't want to answer any more questions about their parents, but they had Alex's interest tweaked now, and he wouldn't rest until he knew what was going on.

They were in the bedroom for quite a while, and then Melissa emerged alone.

"David was sleepy too," she said, "and now I'd better go to bed. If the storm lets up, you can leave first thing in the morning."

She offered him a pillow.

"Will you be comfortable enough with this and the blanket in the big chair?" she asked.

"Look, pal! What's going on here?" Alex demanded. "What are you kids doing here alone? Where are your folks?"

Melissa's brow furrowed. She sank heavily onto a low bench and remained silent.

"All right," said Alex. "I won't press you right now if you don't want to tell me, but is it true that you don't have a phone?"

"Yes," Melissa answered. "We had one, but they came and took it away. We don't miss it."

"Do you go to school?" Alex asked.

"Yes, David and I meet the bus every day down at the overpass."

"What about Emmy? Does she . . .?"

Alex's question was cut short by a low moaning sound. Melissa's eyes widened as she stood and excused herself. She moved quickly to a small door that Alex hadn't noticed before and entered a darkened room.

Alex was right behind her, but she met him at the door and blocked his way. He could see her mature composure falling apart, and suddenly she was very much a little girl. Her once-confident features were now full of fear.

"You can't go in there!" she said sternly, but her voice quivered as she spoke, and Alex knew she was on the verge of tears.

"Now come on, girl! What in the world is going on? Who's in there?" Alex demanded. His patience was fading fast.

Melissa's composure fell completely apart, and she began to sob.

"It's my mother! She's terribly sick! Please don't hurt her!"

Alex's mouth dropped open in surprise. He bent down and took hold of the girl's shaking shoulders.

"Why do you think I'd want to hurt her? I'm a doctor!"

As he gently but firmly moved her aside, he could see that his words had penetrated Melissa to the center of her being.

"A doctor!" she sobbed. "Oh, thank God! I didn't know—I thought . . ."

Alex fumbled and found a light switch on the inside wall by the door. He flipped it on and light instantly filled the small room.

There, in a handcrafted bed, was a beautiful but obviously very sick woman. Her face was flushed and lined with anguish. Her eyes squinted at the light, but she didn't appear to be aware of his presence. Alex lightly touched her face. She was ablaze with fever. He felt for her pulse. It was weak and irregular. Her breathing was shallow and uncertain. She was in need of immediate medical attention. He knew that without it she might not make it through the night.

He judged her to be about his own age or maybe a little younger. She was lovely, even though her illness—and perhaps a hard existence—had left their unmistakable marks.

The questions that filled his mind were instantly replaced with a flood of professional processes. A quick and precise diagnosis was formed from his excellent training and experience. He needed to act immediately. If they'd been in the city, he would have called an ambulance and taken her to a hospital. That was obviously not possible now.

His thoughts centered on the black leather medical bag he always carried in the trunk of his car. The storm raging outside was suddenly of no concern. He had to have that bag, and fast!

"Melissa, I have to go back to my car for medicine. We have to get her temperature down. Get all the towels in the house and wet them with cold water. Place as many of them as possible on her head, neck, and upper body. Rotate them to keep them cold. Can you do that?"

The child's sobbing had subsided. Alex wiped the tears from her eyes and held her face close to his.

"I'm a good doctor, Melissa. She's going to be okay, pal, I promise! I'll be back as soon as

I can. Now get those towels going!"

He reached for his soggy shoes, but Melissa, who had scrambled toward a small closet, tossed out two old, insulated rubber boots and a pair of worn, fleece-lined leather gloves.

"Here, these were my father's. They will help keep you warm."

Alex pulled on the welcome additions, wrapped the big blanket about him, and just before he opened the door, Melissa handed him some matches and told him to use the lantern that was hanging on the wall outside to help him find his way. She also suggested that if the snow was getting too deep, he might want to use the snowshoes.

"You're a good kid, pal," he said. "You keep those cold towels going, and I'll be back soon."

It seemed truly incredible to Alex how motivation compressed time and distance. True, the glow of the lantern and the boots and gloves helped greatly, but there were other even more important reasons why he was able to make the round trip from the house to the car and back again in record time, even though by then the snow was over a foot deep.

Melissa had correctly predicted the closing of the freeway. There was no way traffic could still pass on the Interstate. Alex shuddered at the thought of what would have happened if he had tried to walk out. Although he still hesitated to admit it, he knew that the car—his powerful, showy status symbol—might have caused his untimely demise, that he might have lain an unidentified lump in some snowdrift until the spring thaw. He hoped there was no one else stranded out there as he had been.

The black leather medical bag was right where he'd left it. Among its contents was, indeed, just what the doctor ordered.

Melissa had done her job perfectly. Though her mother's temperature had not dropped, it certainly had not gotten any worse. After he administered the medication and did his best to make his patient as comfortable as possible, he tucked the weary little girl into bed with a promise that he would watch her mom through the night. Then he returned to the mother's room and tended to her medical needs.

Alex sat on the floor and propped himself up in the corner by his patient's bedside. A feeling of professional pride, which he felt was justified, came to the surface. *This will make a great story,* he thought. Doctors Alexander I and II will be proud when they hear about this. That kind of return will more than justify his investment.

Chapter 4

The Day before Christmas

The next thing Alex was aware of was a vigorous shaking of his shoulder.

"Alex, wake up! Breakfast is ready."

He slowly opened his eyes. Emmy grinned at him and wished him a good morning. He tried to get to his feet. Every muscle in his body was rebelling from the ordeal of the night before.

"Oh, I've got to do something to get myself in better shape," he groaned.

He leaned over to study his patient. She was restless and not conscious of anything going on around her. Alex administered more medication and fluffed her pillow. He sensed she was making progress.

As he entered the other room, he was surprised to find that the remarkable crew of little people had been busy. Everything was neat and tidy. The inside of the house sparkled more in the daylight than it did at night.

He went to the window and stared in awe. It was unreal. There must be at least three feet of snow. The wind had subsided, but snow was still falling substantially. The countryside was a wonderland of trackless white. It was doubtful that they would get the freeway open today.

Alex sat at the breakfast table with the children. His too-long neglected stomach growled for attention. The table was neatly set with old-fashioned and oddly matched dishes and silverware. These kids were truly amazing.

Melissa plopped a big spoonful of brown-looking mush into each bowl. The children poured milk on theirs with no sugar, butter, or anything else.

"Is this what I think it is?" Alex asked warily.

"It's cracked wheat. Eat every bit of it," Melissa ordered. "Mother says it sticks to your ribs."

"I'll bet it does," Alex agreed sarcastically. "Is that more of that funny-tasting milk?"

"Sure! It's good for you. David just finished milking Mabel. It's still warm and creamy."

"Is cracked wheat and milk all you kids know how to fix? That's what you were going to feed me last night, too."

Melissa's face lost it radiance.

"I'm sorry you don't like it, Alex. Mother says I'm a really good cook for my age, but since our mother has been sick, that's pretty much the only food we have. But we have plenty of wheat and hay, and Mabel is a really good cow, so we'll be okay until our mom can get better and figure something out."

"That's the only food you have?" Alex asked incredulously. "Gee, I'm sorry, honey," he apologized. "I didn't know things were that tough. I'm sure you're a very good cook, but I really don't have much of an appetite.

My system isn't used to that kind of food."

Melissa said it was okay, but Alex could see that she felt as though his comments were a reflection on her cooking ability. Alex felt genuinely sorry for his insensitivity. How could he have guessed? He'd never known anyone who didn't have more than enough food to eat.

For the second time in the past several hours, Alex's thoughts focused on the contents of his stranded car. Some of that fancy food would surely taste good about now.

"I'll tell you what," he said to the kids. "If David will take a little trip to the car with me, all of us will have a real holiday dinner!"

The quizzical looks on their faces were understandable. After all, where could they possibly go? They were snowed in.

After donning their warm clothes and going outside, David took snowshoes from where they hung on the porch and handed a pair to Alex.

Alex had seen snowshoes before, but he'd

never imagined that one day, in search of food, he'd have to wear a pair into the swirling white fury of a blizzard.

With the help of his boy mentor he did rather well in getting the snowshoes on, but he was in trouble when he tried to take his first step. The snowshoes stayed right where they were while Alex tipped head first into a snowdrift. The kids laughed until they hurt as they dug him out. It was clear to them that it would take a while before he finally got the hang of walking with them. But in the deep snow, it didn't take long for Alex to develop a genuine appreciation for the new additions to his feet.

The car was only visible as a large bump in the snow. It was almost completely buried. They swept the fluffy, feather-like whiteness away from the door on the driver's side. Alex unlocked the door manually, opened it, and folded the seat forward for access to the back seat.

"What do you have in there? " David asked.

"Oh it's just some things I picked up for my family."

Alex didn't elaborate. He could always pick up more canned hams and fruit along the way.

Imagine, Doctor Alexander Pennington III spending the day before Christmas clear out here in the wilds of the West. He wondered if his family would regard this incident with disdain or if they would give him a medal. He found it interesting that he really didn't know which way to call it.

In what seemed like hardly any time at all, Alex and David were back at the house. Between them they carried a full basket with a large cardboard box balanced on top of it. Melissa opened the door for them. They were both huffing and puffing as they put their load on the floor inside.

"Well, my little chef," Alex said to Melissa, "let's see what you can do with this kind of food."

While putting his outer clothing back

into the small closet, Alex watched with amusement as the children unpacked an assortment of foods they had probably never seen or even dreamed of before. They squealed and screamed and giggled with a childlike glee, which Alex found extremely satisfying. This kind of giving was a lot more fun that getting. Why hadn't he ever tried it before? Talk about a return on an investment—and it was a return that was totally unexpected.

The little gathering feasted until they were stuffed, and they enjoyed each other's company at least as much as they did the food. As they ate and rested, they talked about everything. Gradually, the children began talking about their father.

Apparently, at one time, he had been a gentle, hardworking man who loved his wife and children. The older kids still had good memories of him. When Melissa and David were little, they lived in town and their father drove his truck to work on the ranch each day. But their parents had big plans to build a new home on the ranch. They fixed up the little one-hundred-year-old house that they now lived in and moved their family into it to save money. Then their father's National Guard unit was activated and he left home to help fight a war in a far away country. They remembered that they and their mother were very sad to see him go.

When he finally returned, they were all excited. But something was different. Their mother told them it was as though their real father had been killed in a battle, and that his body had come back to them with a very different person inside.

They remembered that she tried very hard to make him happy, but he wasn't really home much after that. They knew that he drank alcohol and took drugs. When he did come home, their mother often had bruises that they could see, and she cried a lot.

They knew that, somehow, he had received a lot of money from the government, and used it to buy more land. They also knew he had sold much of the property to an oil company, and that part of that agreement drilled a well for water and brought electricity in with a guarantee that it would always be provided with no further cost to them from then on.

As time went on, their father sold more and more of the land to support his habits. One night he came home after he had been away for a long time. He stayed just long enough to change his clothes and get all of the money that their mother had saved. She tried to stop him, but he wouldn't listen. He drove away in his pickup truck and two weeks later, the sheriff came by to say that the truck had been found upside down in a gully. Their father's body was still inside. The money was gone. The kids were sorry that they didn't still have all the property, but they were glad that they at least owned everything that they did have, and that no one could take it away from them.

They remembered that creepy people sometimes came around to make deals with their father. Sometimes they would come when he wasn't there and threaten their mother. One time, long after their father's death, one of them grabbed her arm and twisted it so hard it made her cry. When Alex had knocked on their door the night before, they were afraid that one of them had come back. That's why David got out the old shotgun. He had loaded it, too, and fully intended to use it if he had to. He would never let anyone make his mother cry again, especially when she was so sick.

They said they could never remember their mother being so sick before. She had remade all of her warm coats for them. On a very cold night a week or so ago, she went to help David with the chores wearing only an old sweater, and she caught a bad cold. She got worse and worse until she had to go to bed and couldn't get up. Not knowing what else to do, they had been praying and praying for a miracle, just like she had always taught them to do. She also taught them that they must always work like everything depended on them and pray like everything depended on the Lord. She said that kind of team could never be whipped.

Alex's respect for these remarkable little people rose to new level. He asked why, under the circumstances, they had finally decided to let him in.

"Well, we didn't realize at the time that you were the miracle!" Melissa said. "If you were one of the creeps, we didn't care what happened to you. But if you were just a regular person who was in real trouble, mother would have been disappointed in us if we hadn't taken care of you.

"I decided to follow you at a safe distance to see if you were for real. When I found out your car was really broken, my heart told me that we couldn't just let you die out there. Mother has always taught us to be kind and friendly. We wanted to help you, but we were afraid. We decided to let you just stay the night and try to keep mother hidden from you. When she got worse last night, I was really frightened. Now, we are so thankful you came. Heavenly Father sent you to us, and we are glad that he chose you."

Alex was trying not to admit it, but the little girl's sentiment had touched him in a profound way.

"Has the freeway ever been snowed in like this before?" Alex asked.

"Yes, a few times," Melissa answered. "They eventually get it cleared and everyone dug out. Then they come up to check on us. They'll probably be here later today, or maybe tomorrow. With tonight being Christmas Eve, it may take a little longer this time."

"We often have to wear snowshoes to the bus," David said. "It snows quite a bit in the winter."

Alex checked on his patient periodically. He regularly administered medication from the black leather bag. Her discomfort seemed to be lessening, but she remained unaware of anything going on around her. Once she even opened her eyes and seemed almost alarmed to see him there, but he talked to her gently and held her hand, and she drifted again into a fitful sleep.

Gradually the snow began to let up. The peaceful day was one of the most relaxing Alex could remember. He had a hard time thinking of anything he would rather be doing.

Emmy climbed up to the cupboard and found a small ornate metal container.

"Mommy has been saving this all year," she said as she handed it to Alex. "She said we could have it for Christmas Eve. Can we Alex? Please?" He opened the container and was surprised to find that it was filled with popcorn.

Somehow that little can triggered a deep emotion in Alex. He realized that the little mother in the other room was in this predicament in life not by choice or indolence, but by circumstances beyond her control. *Probably no one*, thought Alex, *has ever worked harder to provide a good life and happiness for her children.* He knew that she had done her best to stand by her husband, and under the most trying conditions. It was also clear that she had never turned away from her obligations as a wife and mother. That little container of popcorn said it all. Alex realized that it symbolized the highest form of love for her children and a desire to give them something special for Christmas, even when there was nothing.

He knew, too, that this wonderful little lady would not have just popped the corn for eating. She would have coaxed from it the fullest possible festive value, and that the eating would be the climax.

"Melissa," he said, "does your mom have needles and thread?"

"Yes," she replied, and she hurried to a small old-fashioned-looking wooden cabinet in a corner by the door. When she opened it up, Alex was astounded to see that it was a sewing machine.

"Is that what your mom used to make your coats?" he asked.

"Yes," was Melissa's reply, "and she made other things, too—the curtains, the quilts, the pillows, and even the rugs on the floor."

Alex found himself developing some real feelings for this remarkable lady, as well as for her children.

"Let's really have some Christmas fun with this popcorn," he said. The response was enthusiastic.

Alex and David took the axe from the wood box and the snowshoes and went up on the hill. They cut a small pinion pine for a Christmas tree. They found an old packing box and a few nails in the barn and made a stand for the tree and put it in one corner of the room where the girls had cleared a place. They popped the corn in the large, cast-iron frying pan over the cook stove. They sang Christmas carols and made up nonsensical ditties that totally destroyed their composure. They strung the fluffy popcorn morsels on strands of thread and decorated the little tree. David folded a large paper star for the very top. They draped their popcorn tinsel from the curtain tops and looped it across the massive wooden fireplace mantle. Then all the popcorn that was left over they put into a big bowl in the middle of the rug on the floor, and they nibbled on it while they sat in a circle and cut paper dolls from scrap paper. They made balls, paper airplanes, and other cute and funny shapes and put them all on the little tree.

When they got hungry, they ate clover honey on French and pumpernickel bread and snacked on fruit and ham and cheese. They drank the finest imported chocolate milk that money could buy. Oh, what a Christmas Eve! Alex felt certain that none of them, especially himself, had ever experienced anything like it before. They told stories of Christmas. Some were serious, and some were so hilarious they laughed until it was painful.

If anyone had tried to tell Alex twenty-four hours earlier that he would be where he was and having a genuinely good time—especially with three kids—he would have laughed himself silly. But these kids were different. The day passed quickly, more quickly than any of them realized. It was Melissa who finally went to the window and noticed that night had come. She exclaimed in delight, "Oh, wow! Everybody come and look. It's stopped snowing and the moon is out!"

Emmy ran to the window, and David and Alex opened the door. The sensation was breathtaking. Almost four feet of radiant, untracked snow reflected the light from a brilliant half moon that had climbed high in the sky. It was so bright that the features of the surrounding countryside stood out with clarity. There wasn't even the slightest breeze, and the cold air was so crisp that it stung cheeks and noses, both inside and out. There wasn't a single sound to interrupt the absolute silence. Everyone gathered at the edge of the little porch and drank in the serenity until the cold of the night air forced reality back. In unity, they dashed inside the warm house and huddled around the fireplace. Alex was, once again, aware that his shivering was not entirely from the cold.

Suddenly Melissa gave a quick exclamation, and her hand went to her mouth.

"Oh, oh! Mabel! David, you haven't fed and milked Mabel since early this morning."

Without saying a word, David went to the small closet and began pulling on boots and a scarf, and then his worn, but substantial winter coat.

Once again, Alex was overwhelmed by the maturity of these unselfish children and the magnitude of their undertaking.

"Emmy and I had better do the dishes and clean up this mess before it's time for bed," Melissa said authoritatively. What would you like to do, Alex? Help with the dishes, or help David with the outdoor chores?"

Alex winced at the options he'd just been

given. He'd never done either of them. He smiled, both inwardly and outwardly, at the kind of compliance that was obviously the style of the Stewart family.

"I'll help David," he said. "It looks like we guys had better stick together."

Alex pulled on the big, insulated boots and took down his new leather jacket that had dried stiff from its soaking the night before. He turned up the collar and pulled the lined leather gloves onto his hands. As he went to leave, Melissa called to him.

"Here, take my hat to keep your ears warm!" She tossed him a knitted stocking cap. "Mother makes these, too," she added with a smile.

"Yes, your majesty." Alex smiled with an exaggerated bow. He pulled the warm cap down over his ears and followed the grinning David into the night.

David picked up two buckets that Melissa had just washed and rinsed. One was half full of warm water. David handed that one to

Alex. He stopped on the porch for snowshoes and the old coal oil lamp, which he lit. Then he headed for the small, neat outbuilding.

As they entered the barn, the glow of the lamp filled the enclosure with soft light. The natural aroma of manure and green hay filled the cold air. The big, brown cow lowed softly as the boy moved up to her side. He patted her and said something to her in a quiet tone.

Alex eyed the neatly stacked bales that filled most of the space.

"Where did you get all the hay?" he asked.

"We grew it," came the reply. "We plant it up in the field and the neighbors come and help us cut and bale it. Mom says we might have to sell the field next. I don't know what we'll do then, but we'll work something out."

Where do these kids get their confidence? Alex marveled. *They're always sure that things are going to work out, even when reality is dreadfully bleak.*

David latched a secure grip on the two twine strands that held together a bale that surely outweighed him. With a practiced move he jerked the bale from the stack and landed it squarely in the feeding manger. He took a utility knife from a nail on the wall, and with two quick slices, the bale burst. He safely discarded the twine, spread the hay, and the cow began to munch. Alex was uneasily aware that he wasn't really being that helpful, but he'd never done this sort of thing before. He honestly didn't know what to do.

David seemed to sense his uncertainty, and with a good-natured grin, he picked up on the authoritative tone that had worked so well for his sister.

"Well, don't just stand there, Alex; get that shovel hanging on the wall and scoop up that poop!"

Alex tried to hide a smile that he couldn't control.

"Yes, sir! And where would you like me to put it, sir?" he replied with mock enthusiasm. What else could he say?

"Out in the pile in the back, son," came the

exaggerated deep ten-year-old voice. "Where do you think?"

At that, David lost his assumed composure completely and they both cracked up, giggling and laughing until they could hardly stand up.

Gradually, David got back down to business. As he stroked Mabel's side and talked gently to her, he pulled a low stool up to her and carefully washed her udder with the warm water. He toweled it dry with a clean cloth he had stashed under his coat. Then he placed the milk bucket in position, put his cheek against the cow's side, and began to milk.

In expert style, squirts of milk rhythmically echoed off the bottom of the bucket. Within ten minutes, the container was half full.

Alex watched in amazement. Finally his interest and curiosity overcame his caution and he asked if he could try.

"Sure," came the reply, "If you think you can handle it."

The giggling that followed that comment

was nothing compared to that which followed when Alex sat on the low stool and began to pull.

Mabel shifted uneasily at the inexperienced feel of the newcomer.

"Take it easy, Alex," David chuckled. "You don't pull, you squeeze. Mabel won't like you."

After a few erratic squirts finally hit the bucket, Alex had to yield to the better man. Both agreed that David should finish the job before they lost the whole bucket to Mabel's agitation. The relieved cow seemed to agree.

With the chores completed, David and Alex snowshoed back to the house and, while sharing the load of the full bucket between them, tried to whistle several stanzas of "Jingle Bells," which isn't easy while you're laughing.

The girls had done a beautiful job of tidying up, and Melissa took charge of caring for the milk. She placed most of it in clean bottles in the refrigerator and heated the rest in the large pot for a bedtime snack. Although Alex had gained a healthy respect for the process and was impressed with the cleanliness and care with which the milk was treated, he still couldn't bring himself to drink any.

As the children sipped on the warm refreshment, Melissa quietly went into the room where her mother slept and came back carrying a large timeworn Bible.

"Alex, mother always reads the story of the birth of the baby Jesus to us on Christmas Eve. Would you please read it tonight?"

Alex was at once touched and embarrassed. He had heard the story many times, of course, but he didn't even know where to find it. Melissa was sensitive to his concern.

"It's in the New Testament. The place is marked," she said in a matter-of-fact tone that he'd come to expect from this bunch.

"I'll tell you what," Alex said. "You guys get ready for bed, and then I'll read it to you, okay?"

He was buying a little time for a rehearsal of something he was not too familiar with.

Alex was ready, though, when they

returned. He gathered them around him as he sat in the big chair with the fire blazing in the fireplace, and he was all set to start when Melissa interrupted.

"Before you begin, Alex, we want you to know that we have never had a nicer Christmas Eve. We feel sorry that you can't be with your own family, and we wish our mother could have been able to enjoy it too, but we are so glad that Heavenly Father has brought you to us. While you and David were gone to your car, Emmy and I made this. We wish we had a present to go with it."

She handed him a simple card, handmade with red construction paper. Green holly leaves were pasted in the corners, and carefully printed in black crayon on the cover were the words: "To our best friend, Alex . . ." He opened it. The words continued, "Merry Christmas! We wish you could stay forever! We love you! Your new friends, Melissa, David, and Emily Stewart."

Alex looked away from their penetrating

eyes. Something strange was happening inside him that he wasn't sure about, and he didn't want to let it show.

"Thanks, guys," he finally managed to say in a quiet tone that almost choked him. "I wondered who was responsible for my being here. Now I know who to blame," he said with a slight wink. "And, very seriously," he continued, "I've enjoyed it, too—very, very much. Besides, you are my family, sort of, aren't you?"

The agreement was enthusiastic and unanimous.

Everyone fell silent and looked thoughtful as Alex opened the big, worn book and began to read. He had to blink several times to get the words into focus. Those tears he was trying to hide were now blurring his vision.

"And it came to pass in those days that there went out a decree from Caesar Augustus, that all the world should be taxed . . ."

As the fire died down and the story came to an end, no one seemed to want to break the spell. Finally, Melissa, as always, led the way.

"Good night, Alex. Thank you."

David and Emily both said good night, too, and then Alex witnessed yet another powerful example of love and family unity, the likes of which he had never known. The two younger children quietly followed Melissa into the room where their mother slept and knelt in the darkness at the edge of the big bed. As Alex listened, each, in turn, offered a prayer. Their prayers were simple, sincere, and different, but they all contained two thoughts: please bless mother to get well, and please bless our good friend Alex . . . and thank you for bringing him to us.

Following their prayers, each one gently kissed their sleeping mother and without another word went to their humble bedroom.

Chapter 5

A Struggle with Love

Alex had plenty to think about as he sat back in the comfortable old overstuffed chair. He felt the warmth of the flickering fire on his face. There had been many fireplaces in his life: in ski lodges, majestic mountain retreats, and in his own home in the Eastern United States. In all their fanciness, there wasn't one of them that could match the majesty and gentle, genuine honesty of this fireplace. The structure itself radiated as much warmth as the fire that burned within it. That other, and perhaps more prominent warmth came from the fire of the builder's passion: his love for his family who would dwell in the little home and his need to have them protected and secure. This fireplace was a labor of love that wrapped itself around you.

Alex realized that the other fireplaces of his life, beautiful as they were, were designed and built only to gain a profit. They could never radiate any warmth other than from the physical fire they contained.

What about the Pennington Creed? It was obvious to Alex that some of its tenets were in jeopardy. Was he allowing more than just the professional aspects of this experience to enter into him? And what about the investment? What of a temporal nature could these humble people ever pay him? Where was the required "substantial return?"

His thoughts drifted next to the friendly little Christmas tree. Small as it was, it occupied a rather large portion of the total room and filled the air with a pinion scent. Standing there in its simple décor of thread and paper dolls and popcorn, it, too, radiated warmth and fellowship in a most honest, straightforward way. It was as though the tree, like him, had responded to the invitation to come in out of the cold to this haven of warmth and love, and to also become a member of the family.

Alex contrasted that notion with those of other Christmas trees he had known. Most were tall, stately, and ornate; formal, rigid, and untouchable. As beautiful as they were, they radiated nothing warm but spoke silently and coldly of wealth and power and influence—indeed the kinds of things they were intended to symbolize.

And what about this idea of a miracle? "Miracle" was a word used by the ignorant and superstitious to explain the unexplainable. Innocent, gullible human minds were forever substituting that word for things that could more appropriately be called "coincidence."

His philosophical reverie was gently interrupted when a tiny hand reached out from behind to touch his own as it lay outstretched on the worn arm of the old chair.

"Alex, I can't sleep." It was Emmy. "Can I have a drink of water?"

Alex stood, took her hand in his, and walked to the kitchen corner of the room.

As she drank from a small plastic cup, he was at once enchanted and impressed at how truly delightful and appealing a young child can be. How had he never noticed before? Was this, perhaps, just a special batch of children?

As the child politely thanked him and handed the cup back, he nearly dropped it in surprise as she looked him squarely in the eye and frankly asked," Alex, is my mommy going to die?"

He dropped to his knees beside her. "Not if I have anything to say about it," he said with professional assurance. "Why do you ask that, sweetheart?"

"Well, David and Missy are worried, I can tell. They keep looking at each other funny. They tell me she is just sleepy, but I know she's really sick. Boy, big kids don't think little kids know anything!"

"Yes, punkin, they're worried," he said. "And she is, indeed, really sick, but she is going to be just fine. After all, she's got the best doctor there is looking after her, and he's not going to leave until she is all better, so don't you worry, okay?"

Emmy's big eyes momentarily looked at the floor. "Okay," she mumbled in relief. And then, another question came that he wasn't prepared for. "Alex, do you believe in Santa Claus? David and Missy say he isn't real and that he's just your mom or your dad. But we don't have a dad anymore, and mommy's sick, so he won't be able to come this year."

"My goodness," said Alex, as he sat back on his heels. "Your little head is troubled by some pretty heavy-duty stuff, isn't it? What do you think?"

"Well, I want him to be real, but mostly I just want mommy to get better. What do you think?"

Her trust in him was overwhelming, and it was clear to Alex that she wasn't going to let him off the hook. He was quite sure that she would absolutely believe anything he told her. There had never been anyone like that in his life before. The weight of the responsibility was unlike anything he had ever experienced.

After some serious thought, Alex finally said, "Honey, there are some things that are real, and some things that are pretend, and little girls have the right to pretend and believe in anything they want to, in spite of what the big kids say. Now, the fact that your mom will get better—that's real. You can count on it. As for Santa Claus—well, frankly, before meeting you guys, I hadn't really given it much thought. I suppose some people need Santa Claus to be real more than others do. After tonight, though, I guess I'd believe almost anything."

Alex paused, thought for a while, and then hunkered down to speak face to face with Emmy. "I'll tell you what. Let's you and me have a secret," he whispered. "Let's believe, really hard, that the spirit of Santa Claus is real, and see what happens. Okay?"

"Okay!"

Again those huge, trusting eyes looked to the floor. Emmy's little hands clasped behind her back, and then her big, beautiful, innocent eyes looked directly into his.

"Alex, I love you," she said. "Will you marry me when I grow up?"

Again, that strange, new sensation started swelling from somewhere deep within him, and this time it spread through his entire being. Alex thought to himself that there was no way he would ever saddle such a wonderful little person with a burden such as him. *You deserve someone so much finer than I*—he even tried to say, but somehow the words stuck. They wouldn't come out. His keen, medical mind searched frantically for a physical reason for this new-felt malady, but there was none. He realized for the first time in his adult memory that he was wrestling with the beautiful, debilitating illness called love, for which there was no medicine or known cure. Doctors Alexander Pennington I and II had warned him about that.

Little arms reached about his neck and pulled him close. A little cheek pressed against his. It was the softest and warmest cheek he had ever known. Chills flooded all over him as little lips softly kissed his neck and then turned upward to whisper in his ear.

"Thank you, Alex, for being so nice."

A battle for control raged deep within Alex. He fought valiantly with everything he had ever been taught; the Creed, the money, the power—everything—but he was forced to yield as his rock and iron constitution, piece by piece, was turned to jelly. An unassuming, totally unselfish, and completely dependent little female had him, firmly but gently, in the palm of her tiny hand.

It suddenly dawned on Alex that he was squeezing her so hard that she would surely suffocate, but she didn't seem to mind. He stood and picked her up. Then he sat back in the comfortable old rocking chair. They rocked and he hummed softly until she fell asleep. He held her close for a long time. It was almost as though she had melted into him and they were inseparable.

He became uneasy about a persistent little wish that also kept welling up—that he would, indeed, never have to let her go.

Finally, he slowly rose and quietly moved to the children's bedroom. He knelt beside the bottom layer of the bunk bed and folded back the soft, gray handmade quilt. The old flowered pillowcase and sheets were showing signs of wear, but like the rest of the house, they were fresh and clean.

Alex gently tucked the little girl in beside her sister, as she, too, peacefully slept. He checked on David as he slumbered innocently in the narrow upper bunk. As he brought the covers up around Emmy's dimpled chin, he brushed the brown hair back and gently kissed the little forehead.

Again the flood forced its way up from deep

within him. Look at them. *What a precious lot*, he thought. *So individual, yet all the same. Self-reliant, yet so dependent. So vulnerable. So beautiful. I love you, too. All of you!*

The flood would no longer be contained. Deep inside him a long-forgotten and neglected dam burst under the pressure of pure love. Foreign-feeling tears bathed his stinging eyes and face and tasted salty on his tongue. He shamelessly gave in to sobs, which racked his body as he knelt in the shadows of the little room. Those sobs shook away the crust of years of strict, unforgiving control, the rust of long-neglected, precious elements of self that now were being lubricated. Many of those elements, for the first time ever, were awakened and made fully operational. Surprising to Alex was the awareness that the tears were not from pity or for the plight of these little people, but instead from the pure, unadulterated joy he had come to know through them—a joy that only a giver can know.

Alex was amazed at the ease with which he put aside the thoughts of what would happen if old Doctors Alexander I and II could see him now. There wasn't even any need to take comfort from the knowledge that they would probably never know the way he had "bit the dust" tonight in terms of everything they had so carefully tried to teach him. They wouldn't understand, even if he tried to tell them, any more than he would have understood himself only a few days earlier.

He did feel a strange, unequaled sense of pity, though, but this pity was for those he knew who had never experienced such emotions. Alex sensed that these emotions were so powerful that they might even change a man's entire approach to life.

Alex stood up. He shook his head at the thought of the incredible coincidence that had brought him here. He dabbed at his wet cheeks and eyes with the sleeves of his expensive wool shirt and quietly moved into the other bedroom to check on his patient.

"Boy, this sort of thing could really get to you," he muttered to himself.

He left the door of the small room ajar to provide a dim light that would be enough to see by but not disturb. The sounds of his patient's slow breathing were deep and regular. Dr. Alexander Pennington III smiled in satisfaction. The medication had finally taken effect. She was responding. He gently took her well-formed wrist in his fingertips. The pulse was rhythmic and strengthening.

"Excellent," he muttered. The back of his fingertips lightly touched the shapely cheek and brow. "Well, lovely lady," he softly said, "you're still mighty warm, but I think you're going to pull through."

Alex looked at the woman's striking features. They were reflected in the faces of each of her children. Her own face, even through the veil of illness and the trials of the past several years of her life, showed strength of character, sensitivity, and honesty. How could any man abuse someone with such an innate dignity? He wondered if such a woman could ever be a part of his life. Not likely. Judging from all of the ones he knew, he would probably end up with exactly what he deserved. That was a discouraging thought. He smoothed the bedcovers and looked down at the children's lovely mother, who was also finally sleeping peacefully. "What a story those little kids' behavior tells of you," he said softly.

He felt an unmistakable sense of professional satisfaction. He was a good doctor. Now he, too, wondered whether he could ever be content just doing research. "The world's finest doctor making house calls," he chuckled as he softly shut the door. "Man, this is the ultimate house call!"

The little house was quiet and peaceful and made even more cozy and secure by the conditions he knew were on the outside. Surely tomorrow the realities of life would return. The snowplows would get the highway functional. He would be able to get a tow truck to his car, and his life would return to normal. But, tonight, he would continue to soak up all he could of an experience that he was finding to be not at all unpleasant.

Some interesting dynamics, which he had never been aware of, had been turned loose inside Alex. He was determined to take the fullest advantage of them until the outer world again reached him and caused him to return to his own reality. Although he was sure he could never forget these special kids and their pretty mother, he was equally certain that, with the sun, the callous training and circumstance of that other world he knew too well would return with its unyielding pressures and demands that would never permit him to drift too far astray.

I am too practical, Alex confessed. The world of other values—or lack of them—was too well ingrained. To think they could ever really change was only a romantic notion, and Alex was definitely not a romantic. No, any real change now from his life-long pattern would require a miracle that even the magical forces of Christmas and this special circumstance could not likely pull off. Even if there was a God, Alex was sure that he was so far removed and so buffered by generations of non-compliance to His ways that he was beyond reach.

Although this delightful coincidence in which he now found himself was remarkable (and what would have happened to both him and this little family if coincidence had not intervened?), it was simply that—a delightful coincidence, perfectly rational and explainable. Although it was unusual, it was not miraculous.

The thought that he could possibly become permanently sensitized to the wonderful things he had seen and felt this night was a dream. It was as though he was on a visit to Fantasyland. Alex wasn't anxious to leave, but he knew the time would come that he would have to go home and back to work. He also knew that a person's basic value system, carefully implanted over a lifetime, would stubbornly resist change. His system had not been haphazardly planned. He had been carefully programmed from birth—programmed to achieve someone else's version of success.

No, pragmatics taught him that no matter how delightful and remarkable this experience was, the probability of real change was remote. He could do some things to help these precious people—as indeed he would—but a lasting change in his own life would require a force greater than any he could imagine. It would take a miracle.

Well, enough of that philosophical intro-spection, Alex thought. Weather conditions were not really ideal for an evening stroll, but he again pulled on his new leather jacket, zipped it to the max, turned the collar up to just under his ears, put on the knit cap and everything else he could find to keep him warm, and opened the sturdy door to bright moonlight and bone-chilling cold. He exited the warmth and security of the little haven to make the first of what would become several freezing one-mile round-trip journeys to his shiny new automobile, which was stranded out in the middle of nowhere just on the other side of the freeway overpass.

In the warmth of her bed, a beautiful, trusting little girl dreamed of Santa Claus, and there was no way she was going to be disappointed this Christmas!

Chapter 6

Christmas Morning

"Alex, wake up! He came! He came! We believed and he came!"

Alex blinked his eyes, forced sleep from his brain, and felt himself being pulled upright in the big chair where he had collapsed from his labors just a short time before. It was Emmy, yelling and screaming and jumping about.

She gave up on him and headed back to the little bedroom.

"Missy! David! Wake up! He came!"

"Who came? What are you talking about?" a groggy David mumbled.

"Santa Claus came, dummy! Who else would come on Christmas?"

"What's going on here?" Melissa was finally jarred awake.

"Santa Claus came. Get up!"

"Who came?" Melissa muttered.

"Santa Claus! Santa Claus! Me and Alex believed, and he came! He brought me a huge bear! It even has my name on it! And you have stuff, too!"

"Are you crazy, Emmy?" David said, not believing her.

"Oh, nuts! Okay, if you don't want anything, just stay in bed. See if I care!" Emmy ran back to the bear. The stuffed bear did, indeed, have a piece of paper pinned to it with her name on it.

As David stumbled sleepily into the scene, his eyes focused on the package labeled with his name. He tore off the wrapping, opened the box, and those same eyes snapped open in delighted surprise.

"A jackknife! Oh, brother! Oh my! Missy, a jackknife! Can you believe it? But how . . . who . . . ?"

Melissa was now at her brother's side. They both looked at Alex, who was still struggling to wrench himself from the arms of exhausted slumber. He simply shrugged his shoulders. "Don't look at me," he said. "I was asleep."

"Melissa? David?" A voice came from the small bedroom.

"Mother!" David shouted.

"Mommy!" Emmy cried. "Mommy's awake!"

The children ran into the little room and Alex could hear fast, animated talking. He caught bits and pieces of the conversation that basically contained an abbreviated synopsis of the whole story. He just sat there, mainly because he wasn't sure what he should do.

Presently Emmy came running out. Alex stood as he saw the children's mother, clothed in an old bathrobe and walking slowly with support from her two oldest children, come through the door and into the room.

Suddenly, Alex was acutely aware that he hadn't shaved for three days. His hair and clothes were mussed, and he thought he must be a truly frightening sight. He wanted to speak, but what was he supposed to say?

The mother looked him over warily and glanced about the room at the tree, the decorations, the presents, and then back at him. The children were silent. The worry on his patient's face softened and she broke into a careful smile. "Are you Alex?" she asked.

"I am."

"Well, I'm sure there's a story behind all of this, but I . . ." She was obviously struggling to bring meaning to all of the peculiarity. She looked at the faces of each of her children and read from them volumes of trusted information about this strange, but kindly looking, man in her home. She then seemed to sense that Alex was perplexed, too. Her smile widened into a full grin. She held out her hand.

"Well, hello, Alex. I'm Connie Stewart. Obviously you have met my children. Welcome to our humble home."

She took a step forward and staggered. Alex rushed to her side and helped her into the big chair.

"Let's kind of ease into things, Mrs. Stewart," Alex suggested, sounding very much like a doctor. "You've had quite a battle for the past few days. Let's not overdo it.

She sat back and sighed as she again looked around the room.

"How do you feel?" Alex asked.

"I'm not sure," she responded. "I'm very weak, I know that."

"That's to be expected. You haven't eaten anything for four days. Are you hungry?"

"I'm famished!" she said.

"Wonderful!" Alex observed. "That's a very good sign. Missy, maybe your mom would like some hot chocolate and a grapefruit. What do you think?"

"I can handle it, pal," Melissa said with a wink and a smile.

"Oh, my! Hot chocolate and a grapefruit? That sounds delicious, but how . . . where . . .?"

"We'll explain all of that later," Alex interjected. "Right now, just sit back and enjoy Christmas!

"Is it really Christmas?" Connie asked.

"Yes, and Santa Claus came, too!" Emmy yelled, hugging her big stuffed bear.

"I'm afraid so," Alex said, smiling.

"And are you really a doctor?"

"I am that, too," he said reassuringly, "and I can guarantee that you are in good hands."

"My goodness," the mother remarked, still looking overwhelmed. "I have really been out of it. Thank heaven you were sent to us."

"I keep hearing that," said Alex. "Actually, your wonderful children saved my life. I'm just trying to get even."

With Mother joining in, the circle was now complete. The atmosphere was festive. The presents were all opened and exclaimed over, and clearly much appreciated. Melissa loved her new wristwatch, and she and her mom were pleased with their new blow-dryer. The mother was moved to speechless tears with her beautiful pieces of warm winter clothing that fit as if they were designed especially for her.

Alex winced a little at the thought of having to face his little sister, but that didn't affect the smile in his eyes or the feeling in his heart. He'd make it up to her, and he knew exactly how to do it.

The food was delicious, the fire warm, and the little Christmas tree presided proudly over the joyful occasion. The mother gained strength with each passing hour, and the kids seemed to know that she was greatly impressed by the quality of this kind and gentle man who had come so miraculously into their lives. She listened with interest and laughed and cried alternately as every detail of the story was unfolded.

And as for a truly remarkable Christmas— the agreement was universal!

Chapter 7

The Road Crew

The day with its joyful sharing was so peaceful that the loud knock on the door seemed abrupt and intrusive.

"It must be the road crew," Melissa observed. As David opened the door, he was greeted by a hearty, friendly sounding voice.

"Well, hello, David! Is everything okay up here?"

"Hi, guys," David responded in his straightforward manner. "Yes, we are very well, thank you. Will you come in?" Then over his shoulder he added, "Mom, it's Mr. Harvey and Mr. Jenkins from the road crew, and a state trooper.

"No thanks," the good-natured male voice said. "We have snow all over our boots. We're just checking up on you."

Alex glanced through the window and saw a serious-looking four-wheel drive unit with a snowplow on the front. Parked behind it was an ice-covered highway patrol cruiser. He couldn't see the man at the door, but two other men stood waiting in the snow. One wore the heavy-duty insulated overalls of a winter highway crewman, and the other wore the uniform of a state highway trooper. To say that Alex felt they were intruders into the idyllic scene would probably be a stretch, but it can truthfully be said that he didn't feel the surge of relief that two days before he had expected he would.

"Do you know who owns that fancy vehicle down on the off ramp?" the trooper asked. "We saw a beaten path in the snow between there and here."

"Yes, we do," David said. "It belongs to our friend, Alex. It's broken, so he's staying with us until he can get it fixed."

"Is he here now?" the trooper asked authoritatively.

"Yes, I'm here," Alex said as he stepped past the Stewarts and walked through the doorway. "That's my car—at least what's left of it."

"Are you Doctor Alexander Pennington?" the trooper asked.

He not only looks like a trooper, Alex thought, *but he talks like one too.* They had obviously checked the registration.

"Doctor Alexander Pennington the Third," Alex corrected, responding to an impulse he felt to keep the conversation light.

"You're a wanted man, Dr. Pennington," the Trooper grinned as he offered a handshake. "I'm sergeant Will Madsen of the highway patrol. Your family is going crazy trying to find you. They haven't heard from you for three days, and they have an all-points bulletin out for you. The call came from their governor, himself, so we thought we'd better get right on it.

Alex relaxed. *I like this guy,* he thought, smiling inwardly. *He isn't as stiff as I thought he was.*

"Well, don't get too impressed with that governor thing," Alex said. "He and my dad go way back. They were undergrad roommates, and now they're golfing buddies. I tried to call my folks, but my cell phone was dead and the satellite phone must have croaked with every other electronic gizmo in my car."

"We notified your people that we found your vehicle," the Trooper continued, "but the fact that you weren't in it probably caused more angst than it eased. I'll call this in. They'll be relieved to know you're alive and well and being well taken care of."

"Well, actually, it's the other way around," Connie Stewart broke in. "He's the one who's been taking care of us. Thank heaven he came when he did."

"The highway should be open in about an hour," Mr. Harvey said. "We have our section finished. We've been working on it all night and all day yesterday."

"What a way to spend Christmas," Alex observed.

"That's true, but that's the way it goes when you have a job like ours," Mr. Harvey grinned. "It's okay, though. When you get to help someone out, it makes it all worthwhile."

"Do you plow the road up here regularly?" Alex asked. "Or am I the reason you did it this time?"

"Well, don't let this get out," Mr. Harvey said, jabbing the trooper playfully with his elbow, "we're not supposed to leave the Interstate. But with Mrs. Stewart being a widow and all . . . well, we just like to check on her and the kids when we get into a storm like this one. Our section ends a couple of miles beyond the overpass, and it doesn't take much to push a lane through so the kids can get to the school bus."

"That's very kind of you," Alex said. "These people are worth the effort. I'm personally grateful to know that they are being looked after."

"You know, if your car's problem isn't too serious, I have a kid on one of my trucks who's a mechanical wizard. He can fix anything on wheels."

"Oh, I'm afraid I'm out of luck on this one." Alex said. "I'm thinking it's something major."

"It may not hurt to check before we bring a tow truck all the way out here on Christmas," Trooper Madsen pointed out. "This guy works on all our personal vehicles. He's really pretty good."

"I wouldn't want to inconvenience you any more than I already have," Alex said, "but I also wouldn't want to bother anyone else on Christmas; so I guess it wouldn't hurt to check."

"Good," said Mr. Harvey. "He's down there now. I'll get him on the radio."

The radio call was made from the waiting truck, and Mr. Harvey handed the microphone to Alex, who described the car's sudden complete power failure to the mechanic.

"It may not be as serious as it seems," the mechanic responded. "We'll take a look."

"Thank you," said Alex. "I'll see if Mr. Harvey will bring me down with the key pad," he said.

"No need," the mechanic came back. "We just found it in the keyhole in the door. You must have forgotten and left it there."

Alex felt his pockets. Sure enough, he must have been so exhausted on that final trip last night that he didn't even think about keys. He shrugged. "Oh well, no one could have stolen it anyway in the condition it's in," he said.

"I'll call you back in a minute and let you know what we find," said the mechanic.

"Thanks very much." Alex handed the microphone back to Mr. Harvey. "That's awfully nice of you fellows," he said.

"Glad to do it!" Mr. Harvey said. "After

all, it's Christmas, isn't it? We can't leave a man stranded out in the middle of nowhere for Christmas."

The three children and their mother had just begun to relate the story of the past few nights to Mr. Harvey when the radio in his truck again crackled to life.

"Mel? This is Mike. Is that fellow who owns the car still there?"

"Yes, he's right here. I'll put him on."

"Yes, Mike, how bad is it?" Alex asked anxiously.

"Well, it's actually not bad at all," the mechanic said. "It was pretty clear the battery was dead, so we gave it a jump-start and it took right off."

Mel Harvey looked at the stunned Alex, whose eyes widened at the good news.

"That's incredible," Alex muttered. "It was a complete power failure. Absolutely nothing worked. No engine, no lights, no horn . . . nothing!"

"We don't have the equipment out here

to verify it," the mechanic said, "but our best guess is that the chip that directs the flow of electricity from the alternator to the battery went bad, and for a while you were just running on battery power. With the headlights and other equipment on, it couldn't last long and finally just ran out of juice. When the engine quit, you just coasted up the hill."

"That's incredible," Alex muttered, inwardly more than for anyone else to hear. "Does it move now?" he asked.

"Yes it does," the mechanic answered with a smile in his voice. "We dug her out and drove her down to the freeway and back, and she runs fine. That's a fine automobile," he added almost adoringly. "She runs like a three-hundred dollar watch!"

"What will it take to replace the bad chip?" Alex asked with a touch of awe in is voice.

"No need," the mechanic came back. "I put a meter on it and I guess with the jump-start and all, it got bumped back into position. We have the battery charger on it now, and it's taking a charge like a hungry piglet on a sow. By the time you get here, it will be ready to go."

"Could it happen that suddenly, right at that particular off-ramp?" Alex asked in wonder.

"Well, it obviously did," the mechanic said, "and considering all of the random places it could have happened, you're lucky it did."

"But why in that particular spot?" Alex asked persistently, like he was trying to apply reason to something that went far beyond mechanics.

"Well," the kid on the other end said simply, "it looks to me like either you really needed that warm little house or someone in it really needed you. Maybe both! Everything considered, I'd say it's a miracle!"

A miracle! There was that word again. Alex silently mouthed the word, but somehow it had a different feel this time.

"It *was* a miracle," he repeated aloud.

Then he didn't say anything. He couldn't.

He looked like he may be having a brain cramp. Something terribly significant was happening inside him.

Finally, after several awkward seconds, Mike the mechanic broke the silence. "Well, she's right here on the on-ramp ready to go any time you are, sir . . . sir . . . are you still there?"

"Oh, yeah; thanks, Mike. Thanks very much!" Alex finally managed to say. He still stared distantly as he handed the microphone back to Mr. Harvey. "How much do I owe you?" he asked blankly.

"Nothing," the roadman answered. "That's our job. Besides, being stuck clear out here for two nights, especially for Christmas, you've already paid your price, wouldn't you say?"

"Oh, no my friend, quite the contrary!" Alex was regaining his composure. "I owe this little family big time. They saved my bucket in more ways than you would ever guess."

"If you'd like to get your things, I'll be glad to give you a ride back down to your car," the roadman offered. "Although from the trail in the snow it looks like you know the way pretty well by now."

"I appreciate that very much." Alex said as his whole countenance brightened. "But I have a better idea. You and your guys have been working all night, and I'll bet you haven't had breakfast. With Mrs. Stewart's permission, the kids and I can mix up a steaming pot of cracked wheat cereal with real clover honey and warm milk right out of the cow! What do you say? I know I sure could use some!"

His eyes caught Melissa's surprised look and they both winked.

The little family and their hungry road-crew guests, including the state trooper and Mike, the mechanic, crowded into the small house around a radiant old fireplace with a festive pinion pine Christmas tree in one corner, and they feasted. The meal of cracked wheat and clover honey, and fresh milk still warm right out of the cow, couldn't have been more satisfying or eaten with more gusto if it had been pheasant under glass, served in the great hall of a castle to a king and his court!

As a result, the exclusive New England family of Pennington will never be the same. I mean, just imagine the social impact of having your carefully monitored numbers suddenly increased by four—and a cow! And that a significant part of your group was now enjoying a new family tradition: journeying for the holidays to an isolated, humble ranch house in the western hills and eating, of all things, cracked wheat for Christmas!

And while you're imagining, consider the shock of learning that the sacred Pennington Creed had not only been violated in every conceivable way, but had been totally replaced by an opposite approach to life that was now being joyfully referred to by its creators as The Christmas Creed.

About the Author

Ted Collins Hindmarsh was born and raised in Provo, Utah. He is married to Shirlene Rasmussen, also from Provo. They have two daughters and three sons and a growing number of grandchildren and great-grandchildren.

Ted holds two degrees from Brigham Young University—a BS in print journalism and an MA in educational communication. After forty-four years of full-time service, he retired from BYU, where his career included Educational Media Services, Learning Resource Centers, the Freshman Academy program, and the Honor Code office. He was also an adjunctive faculty member of the

BYU communications department for thirty-five years.

Ted is an Eagle Scout, and he was awarded the Silver Beaver for his adult service in Scouting. He has held a variety of church and community youth leadership positions, including Cubmaster, Scoutmaster, youth mentor, and LDS bishop.